Growing GREEN

URBAN GARDENING

by Carol Hand

LERNER PUBLICATIONS · MINNEAPOLIS

Content Consultant: Dr. Shahla Ray, Indiana University,
School of Public Health, Department of Applied Health Science,
Bloomington, Indiana

Lerner Publications Company
A division of Lerner Publishing Group, Inc.
241 First Avenue North
Minneapolis, MN 55401 USA

For reading levels and more information, look up this title at
www.lernerbooks.com.

Library of Congress Cataloging-in-Publication Data

Hand, Carol, 1945- author.
 Urban gardening / by Carol Hand.
     pages cm.—(Growing green)
 Includes bibliographical references.
 ISBN 978-1-4677-9390-2 (lb : alk. paper)—ISBN 978-1-4677-9709-2
(eb pdf)
1. Urban gardening—Juvenile literature. I. Title. II. Series: Growing
green.
 SB457.H33 2016
 635.09173'2--dc23
                        2015013525

Table of CONTENTS

CHAPTER 1
Getting Into Gardening 4

CHAPTER 2
Starting a Garden 16

CHAPTER 3
Why Grow a Garden? 28

CHAPTER 4
Challenges of Gardening 38

CHAPTER 5
Gardening Trends 48

Working as a Community Farm Director 60
Glossary 61
Source Notes 61
Selected Bibliography 62
Further Information 63
Index 64

1

GETTING INTO GARDENING

During the spring and summer of 2014, a garden bloomed in the courtyard of Mount Pleasant Elementary School (MPE) in Livingston, New Jersey. Parent volunteers and MPE Counselor Jennifer Kelner conceived the garden idea, and the school embraced the thought of teaching students about healthful eating and gardening. The goal was to show students where food comes from, prompt kids to try new foods, and give them a hands-on gardening experience.

Together, students, parents, teachers, and the principal obtained a grant from a local farmers' market, as well as a donation of lumber. Several volunteer families built six raised beds in an unused courtyard, and a landscaping company volunteered to clean the space, move soil, and prepare the garden beds.

Students quickly became involved. They chose to plant foods that grow well in New Jersey, including tomatoes, eggplant, basil, corn, chives, peas, and yellow squash. Students brought recycled containers to use as starting pots. They planted seeds, watched them grow into seedlings, and

Recycled containers, such as cans, serve as great starting pots for plants.

then planted them in the garden beds. Counselor Kelner and parent Jodi Rothfeld planned lessons and led classes in gardening. Students learned about plant life cycles, healthful eating, sustainability (using resources so they are not depleted), and horticulture (growing and managing garden plants). During the summer, more than twenty volunteer families cared for the garden, with the kids thoroughly involved in watering, weeding, and harvesting. When school started again, students and teachers harvested the many vegetables.

The MPE garden started small, but the enthusiasm of students, teachers, and parents was contagious. Parent involvement made it a community garden, and plans quickly evolved to extend the growing season into the spring, fall, and winter so that all students—not only summer volunteers—could participate. In 2015, the MPE garden was selected as one of twenty winners of the Youth Garden Grant, sponsored by the Kids Gardening division of the National Gardening Association. This grant donates money, tools, plants, and supplies to winning gardens to ensure that their gardening projects can continue.

Gardening projects such as the MPE garden are on the rise. Gardens produce healthful and delicious fresh foods. Even though gardening is hard work, it is also great fun, and it teaches many skills, making gardeners more self-sufficient.

Early American Farms and Gardens

Since people began settling into villages, they have grown gardens. Through trial and error, they learned which plants grew well in their particular soil and climatic conditions. They often developed a deep knowledge of these plants and used this knowledge to improve their gardens. For example, the Iroquois nation of the northeastern United States used companion planting—growing plants with complementary characteristics together—in their "three sisters" gardens.

THE THREE SISTERS

When European settlers arrived in America in the early 1600s, the Iroquois had been planting three sisters gardens for more than 300 years. The Iroquois discovered important, practical reasons for growing corn, beans, and winter squash together. The tall corn plants serve as poles for bean plants to climb. Bean roots add nitrogen to the soil, fertilizing the corn. Squash mulches, or covers and protects, the soil around the corn and bean plants. Although mulches are often dead organic materials, such as decaying leaves or straw, the huge leaves of living squash work well too. They provide insulation, meaning water is retained, sun does not bake the soil, and weeds cannot grow. At the end of the season, the dead squash plants can be left in place to add nutrients to the soil. In these ways, the three plants thrive together, improve the soil, and make the gardener's work much easier. When grown together, the plants require less weeding and watering. Letting the beans grow upward means there is no need to bend to pick them. There is less need to fertilize because the bean plants and remains of all plants add nutrients and organic matter to the soil. Together, the three sisters make a nearly complete human diet—beans provide protein, corn provides carbohydrates, squash provides vitamins, and squash seeds and corn provide oil.

Before the Industrial Revolution, most European Americans were farmers. Farms in the 1800s were small, producing small amounts of many crops. Farm families planted gardens and raised chickens, cattle, and hogs, some of which they butchered for meat. Except for flour, salt, and sugar, farmers grew all the food they needed to feed their families.

Families planted vegetables and fruits in excess to ensure they had enough food to last through long winters. To prepare for winter, they harvested and canned. They saved seeds from year to year to ensure they had seeds to plant, and they tried various seed types to determine what grew best on their farmland. Many staple food crops in the mid-1800s were root crops, including potatoes, beets, rutabagas, parsnips, and turnips. Root vegetables are large, and because they are rich in carbohydrates and nutrients, they are very filling. This was important to farm families, who worked hard and had little food except what they grew. Root crops also

Many farmers and gardeners still preserve excess produce by canning it.

PRESERVING FOOD BY CANNING

An important aspect of gardening is learning to safely preserve food so the food is not contaminated by food-borne diseases. Before refrigeration was widely available, canning was the main method of food preservation. It is still used extensively. For example, any supermarket food in a can or jar was preserved by canning. In canning, food is placed in jars, and air is removed to create a seal that prevents bacteria from entering. The jars are then heated to kill any bacteria already present.

store well. They require no preparation, such as canning, and can simply be left in a basement or root cellar and brought out, ready to cook, in winter.

The Rise of Industrial Farming

In the late nineteenth and early twentieth centuries, farming changed as machines replaced human and animal labor. More technological advances—many of them in chemistry—led to the development of industrial agriculture, or the production of food on very large, single-crop farms, which began to flourish around 1950. Large chemical plants began producing nitrogen and phosphorus fertilizers in the late 1930s and 1940s. Chemicals developed for the military gave rise to an array of pesticides designed to destroy insect, fungal, and weed pests.

Industrialization and burning fossil fuels contribute to global warming, one of the twenty-first century's most serious problems.

These changes soon transformed farming into an industry. Farming required fewer, but more specialized, workers. As a result, many small farmers began retiring, and homesteads were abandoned. As more people left their farms, and their children settled in cities and suburbs, much of the

US population lost contact with the land. Supermarkets, not family gardens, became the main source of food.

The rise of industrial farming also brought about an unexpected problem. The use of tractors and other farm machinery, combined with the rise in fertilizer and pesticide use, led to an ever-increasing use of fossil fuels. Burning fossil fuels causes severe environmental pollution, including the release of greenhouse gases into the atmosphere. Ten percent of greenhouse gas emissions can be directly traced to agriculture, and the transportation required to move the crops contributes even more.

Early Urban Gardens

Urban gardens became common throughout the early twentieth century, particularly in large cities. During World War I (1914–1918), they were called Liberty Gardens because they supported the war effort. The countries of Europe were all part of the war zone and were unable to produce food for their own people. North America became responsible for feeding its own citizens and those of Europe as well—approximately 120 million people. Food was rationed in both Europe and North America. Prices rose. Americans cut back on the food they bought, and President Woodrow Wilson urged US citizens to grow gardens to feed themselves so that more processed food could be sent to Europe. Liberty Gardens began springing up in communities across the country.

During the Great Depression of the 1930s, depression relief gardens sprouted, helping support hungry and struggling people in the United States. Similar to Liberty Gardens, Victory Gardens supported the World War II (1939–1945) effort. Again, encouraging citizens to grow their own

The US government's War Food Administration created the Victory Garden Program during World War II, urging citizens to help supply food.

food made more commercial food available for soldiers. Because more food was grown at home and less was transported by rail, railroad transport was freed for transporting war supplies. Finally, because citizens were growing

Gardening is one way to combat pollution and improve Earth's living conditions.

much of their own food, they could preserve their own excess food for later use in case of shortages. The success of all these urban garden programs provided a model for twenty-first-century community gardens.

Environmentalism

In the late 1960s, the idea of environmentalism excited many people in the United States. Environmentalism advocates for the preservation, restoration, and improvement of the natural environment—for example, pollution control and wise use of natural resources. Many people understand that they can also help maintain and improve the environment through fairly simple actions, including gardening.

According to census data, 80.7 percent of the US population lived in cities as of 2010. These urban dwellers are finding ways to grow gardens, just as their forebears did. In the twenty-first century, gardeners and homesteaders are looking for ways to meet modern challenges, such as urban poverty, unhealthful foods, and worldwide environmental problems.

Case In POINT

THE EVOLUTION OF HOMESTEADING

The term *homesteading* originally referred to people taking advantage of the 1862 US Homestead Act, which gave free land to European settlers and encouraged them to settle the western United States. They uprooted themselves, moved west, and became farmers. In the twenty-first century, homesteading involves a change in philosophy more than a change in location. It describes anyone who embraces the concept of self-sufficiency. Modern homesteaders do not need to leave the city or suburbs. They use less energy, eat (and often grow) nutritious local foods, and make choices that improve their quality of life regardless of where they live. Rather than taking advantage of mainstream electric and gas systems, they often use alternative energy sources such as solar or wind power. They do not necessarily earn a living by growing produce or making crafts, although they may.

STARTING A GARDEN

Gardens express their owners' creativity. A gardener might have a pot of herbs on a windowsill, a backyard garden, or a country mini-farm complete with chickens and honeybees. Many are organic because gardeners want to raise safe, nutritious foods. Organic gardeners grow food without using synthetic fertilizers and pesticides. They believe that by gardening organically, they are leaving future generations a safer and healthier world. They are in the forefront of the sustainability movement, which promotes the protection of Earth's environment and natural resources. Methods such as composting, companion planting, and using beneficial insects to control pests help gardeners grow lush crops while still being sustainable.

Small, Simple Gardens

There are many different kinds of gardens. The smallest, simplest gardens are container gardens. A container garden may consist of one container or many. A container is anything that holds soil and water. It may sit in the

Gardens vary according to the gardener's interests and tastes and the amount of space available.

PLANNING A FIRST GARDEN

"Growing food is very simple," says Kathleen Frith, managing director of the Center for Health and the Global Environment at Harvard Medical School. "It takes a little time, but things like tomatoes, lettuce, peppers—basic kitchen crops—are very forgiving." Frith gives these tips for starting a first garden:

- Start small. Plant crops you really like.

- Choose a location with at least six hours of good sunlight per day and access to water.

- Do soil tests to ensure your soil has no contaminants.

- If possible, use a raised bed to control the soil and nutrients.

- Ask other gardeners what grows well in your area.

corner of an apartment or fill an entire patio or deck. Containers can be fancy flowerpots, hanging baskets, window boxes, metal cans, wooden tubs, or even old boots. This type of gardening is excellent for small spaces and is easy to tend. Gardeners can move containers to different locations to provide the best conditions of sun, shade, and water. Many plants grow well in containers, including flowers and single tomato plants.

Kitchen gardens grow edible plants to use for cooking and can also be small and simple. Sometimes gardeners grow vegetables for their favorite dishes. A salad garden might contain leafy plants such as spinach, cress, and lettuce. For color and crunch, it might also include radishes, green onions, carrots, and—given enough space—tomatoes and cucumbers. A salsa garden usually contains tomatoes, jalapeño peppers, cilantro, onions, and garlic. Many gardeners grow cooking herbs, including basil, thyme, oregano, parsley, chives, and dill. People often grow herbs in individual pots in a kitchen window or on a deck or patio.

Backyard Gardens

Backyard gardeners have more space than apartment dwellers and can therefore grow more vegetables. They can adjust the garden's size based on the space available and the time they have to tend it. By carefully choosing vegetables and using mulches to cover the soil, hold water, and add nutrients, gardeners can decrease watering, eliminate the need to loosen up soil by tilling it, and minimize weeds and insect pests.

An in-ground garden is planted on flat ground, with no raised beds or containers. This means start-up costs are low. If beds are walked on, however, soil becomes compacted and less productive. Many gardeners have switched to raised beds. These wooden or plastic boxes are placed on the ground and filled with lightweight soil and compost or decayed

Because raised-bed gardens are more exposed to warm air and sunlight, they warm up quickly, lengthening the growing season.

In-ground garden soil must be tilled every spring.

organic matter. No one walks in them, so the soil does not compact. Raised beds also have good drainage, meaning water can flow through without eroding the soil, and the soil never needs to be tilled. The gardener can buy special planting mixes of dirt for easier planting and weeding. Finally, raised beds warm up earlier in the spring. There is less soil in the bed than in the ground, and the soil is lighter, so it is easier for warm air to travel through it.

In a square-foot garden, a typical raised bed is divided into 1-foot (0.3-meter) squares for planting. Large plants, such as tomatoes or peppers, are planted one per square foot. Smaller plants fit four, nine, or sixteen to a square. For example, sixteen carrot or radish plants will grow in one

GROW A PIZZA GARDEN

To grow a pizza garden, use a variation of the square-foot garden. Place a stake in the ground in the middle of the growing area. Attach a 3.5-foot (1 m) piece of string. Hold the string taut, walk in a circle, and mark the garden's boundary with rope, rocks, landscape edging, or whatever you have handy. Fill the circle with about 6 inches (15 centimeters) of good soil or growing mix. Divide it into six equal wedges and grow a different pizza ingredient in each. Plant two or three plants each of oregano, parsley, and sweet basil. Plant up to thirty red, white, or yellow onion sets. Plant one or two sweet bell peppers and one Roma tomato plant. Check your garden daily. Mulch with straw or other organic matter when the plants grow large enough. Water when necessary, and pull out any weeds that appear. If you mulch, there should be very few. Soon you can harvest your vegetables and use them to make a homegrown pizza.

square. Similar to a raised bed, a square-foot garden can be any size, as long as it is divided into 1-foot squares. A well-composted square-foot garden can produce a very high yield of vegetables—much more than a typical in-ground garden. It typically has better soil, is kept well mulched, and is less compacted. Also, in a square-foot garden, plants are properly spaced.

Community Gardens

A community garden is a piece of land that is gardened by a group of people. Land for community gardens comes from different places, often abandoned vacant lots or parcels of land donated by a church, business, or individual. Volunteers run many community gardens, although a few are supported by a city and have paid staff. Community gardeners may use

the produce themselves or donate it to local agencies, such as food banks.
Food banks are nonprofit organizations that collect donated or surplus
food and supply it free or at low cost to people in need.

Workplace gardens are sponsored by a specific company and located on
the company's grounds. Employees grow and use the produce. Community
organizations also grow gardens. Hospitals might use the produce to
provide healthful meals for patients. Museums often set up educational

Often, a community garden is divided into plots, with each gardener or family
caring for a single plot.

START A COMMUNITY GARDEN

If you lack room for a garden, and there is no community garden nearby, consider starting your own. Here are some ideas to get you started:

- Decide on the purpose and goals of the garden. What do you want to accomplish? Who will get the food?

- Find people to help. Talk to friends, parents, teachers, and community members. Set up meetings to make plans. Work as a team or community.

- Plan the garden. Will you divide it into small plots and charge each gardener a fee or work together to grow large amounts of a few crops? What crops will you grow?

- Find a location. Perhaps someone (an individual, a business, or an organization) will donate land, or the city will donate a vacant lot.

- List anyone who might donate start-up funds, for example gardening centers, lumberyards, or businesses. Develop a pitch describing the proposed garden, why the community needs it, and how the donor will benefit. Visit each group and ask for funds.

- After you obtain land and funds, map out the garden. Work together to build beds and other structures. Plan your crops.

- Discuss who will tend the garden and when. Who will mulch, water, weed, and harvest the plants?

programs on gardening and plant care. School gardens are also becoming popular. Cafeteria staff can use fruits and vegetables in school kitchens to add fresh ingredients to school lunches.

Things to Consider

Once you've chosen a garden plot and it is ready, the first step is to decide what to grow. Choose vegetables you like, determine their light, space, and soil requirements, and make sure you have those conditions. For example, a tomato plant needs bright sunlight, plus plenty of air and water. It will require less space and encounter fewer diseases if it is staked or supported. Salad greens, in contrast, are cool-weather crops. They remain small and require less light and lower temperatures than tomatoes.

It's also important to know whether a vegetable produces only one time (such as carrots, radishes, and corn) or multiple times throughout the season (such as tomatoes, peppers, and squash). One tomato plant might provide plenty of tomatoes, while many carrot seeds would be needed to grow the same amount of produce. Finally, some people want only enough vegetables for a summer harvest. Others want excess to preserve for winter. This decision should be made before planting. Otherwise, in August, the gardener may be buried in zucchini with no idea what to do with it.

Feeding Plants

Plants need nutrients to grow. They obtain nonmineral nutrients (hydrogen, oxygen, and carbon) from air and water. Required mineral nutrients occur in soil, dissolve in water, and are taken up by plant roots. Gardeners supplement soil nutrients by adding fertilizers. Fertilizers also replenish nutrients that growing plants take from the soil. But fertilizers do not compensate for factors such as poor soil preparation, lack of water, or weeds.

Instead of throwing away fruit and vegetable scraps, add them to your own compost to make an organic fertilizer.

The two types of fertilizers are organic fertilizer, such as compost, and inorganic, or artificial, fertilizer. Some people describe inorganic fertilizer as *chemical*. This misleading term suggests compost is not composed of chemicals. Everything on Earth is made of chemicals. The difference between organic and inorganic fertilizer is where the chemicals come from and which types of chemical nutrients they contain.

WORM COMPOSTING

Red wigglers, a type of small earthworm, create compost. They can live in the kitchen or classroom, or on the patio. They eat fruit and vegetable scraps (not meat or animal products) and break them down into plant nutrients. Setting up a worm bin requires a shallow, covered box and moist newspaper strips for bedding. The worms need moisture, air, darkness, and warm temperatures. Plastic worm bins are available, but any shallow, covered, plastic or wooden container lined with a garbage bag will work. If you use a tightly covered plastic storage container, poke a few air holes in the top. When considering how many worms to get, the typical suggestion is 1 pound (0.5 kilogram) of worms for each square foot. Just feed the worms, keep them moist, and add bedding as needed. Within three to five months you will have rich compost. To harvest it, move bin contents to one side and add fresh newspaper and food scraps to the other side. After the worms move into the new food, remove the compost.

Organic fertilizer, such as compost, is made directly from the breakdown of decaying animal and plant matter, meaning it contains all the mineral nutrients plants need. Organic gardeners mix compost with garden soil or potting mix when making a new garden bed. They also add compost to beds during every growing season. Inorganic fertilizer is processed. Some of its ingredients are artificial; others come from natural mineral deposits. Inorganic fertilizers contain varying concentrations of nitrogen, phosphorus, and potassium—the three nutrients plants need in the greatest quantities.

Organic fertilizers contain more types of nutrients but have lower nutrient levels than chemical fertilizers. They release their nutrients slowly, just as plants receive them in nature. Compost improves soil texture and water movement through the soil. Organic fertilizers must be properly composted before application. This is particularly true for manure-containing fertilizers, because raw manure can damage plants by releasing harmful salts and weed seeds into the garden. Inorganic fertilizers act much more quickly but are soon lost from the soil and may have to be reapplied several times. Gardeners can measure the amount of inorganic fertilizer, but they often add too much, which burns the soil and plants. Unlike compost, inorganics do not contain all the nutrients plants require, and they do not improve soil texture.

Twenty-first-century gardening encompasses many goals, crops, and techniques. But in general, gardeners seek to grow good healthful food, grow it locally using environmentally sustainable methods, and make themselves and their communities healthier and happier in the process.

WHY GROW A GARDEN?

Some benefits of gardening are personal, such as producing healthful, tasty food and improving mental and physical health. Some are community or social benefits, such as providing food for those in need or building community cooperation. Other benefits are economic, such as saving money on food, or environmental, such as saving energy and decreasing carbon emissions. Most gardens will deliver several or all of these benefits to the gardeners, their families, and their communities.

Healthful Food and Food Security

One major benefit of gardening is producing safe, healthful food. If grown organically, garden food is free of industrial pesticides, unlike food grown on industrial farms. Organic food also contains no additives or preservatives. Food additives, such as artificial colorings, high-fructose corn syrup, and artificial sweeteners, are substances added to processed food, such as canned soup and frozen dinners, to make it more attractive or change its taste. Preservatives are added to extend shelf life or make

Perhaps the biggest benefit of gardening is the fresh foods it supplies.

KITCHEN SCRAP GARDENING

In summer or winter, plants can be grown indoors from kitchen leftovers. Not all of these plants will produce edible foods, but they make beautiful, inexpensive houseplants that freshen the air and beautify your home. Plant three or four seeds from a citrus fruit—orange, lemon, lime, or grapefruit—in a 4-inch (10 cm) pot. After they sprout, keep them well watered for approximately six weeks, then transplant them into separate pots, where they will eventually grow into small trees. In several years, they might bear fruit. To grow an avocado plant, let an avocado seed dry out for several days. Plant it in a pot of well-moistened soil with its top exposed to air. Although these are all tropical plants, they grow well outdoors during warm summers in any climate. Just remember to bring them indoors when the weather starts to cool!

the product last longer. Because organic produce is usually fresh, it tastes better. And because it contains all the vitamins and minerals required for good nutrition—but no potentially harmful substances—most people consider it healthier to eat.

Good nutrition is required for good health, disease prevention, and healthy growth. The dietary guidelines for Americans recommend two to five cups of fruits and vegetables per day (approximately four to ten servings). Home and community gardens provide fresh fruits and vegetables. When people have access to fresh garden produce—particularly if they helped grow it—they eat more of it, and their nutrition improves. They are also more likely to eat a wider variety of vegetables and fruits.

Not everyone has access to healthful foods. According to the US Department of Agriculture (USDA), food insecurity occurs when a person lacks access to the amount of food needed to actively live a healthy life. In 2012, a report from the antihunger group Feeding America stated that 49 million US citizens suffer from food insecurity. One-third of these people are children, and the problem is getting worse. Food insecurity is highest in rural counties in the southern and western United States and in inner cities. Another type of food insecurity is lack of nutritious food, such as fresh fruits and vegetables. People in this situation often eat high-calorie, low-nutrition foods that lead to obesity. Low-income and minority populations, particularly in urban areas, often lack automobiles or access to public transportation. This means they cannot travel to supermarkets to buy fresh foods. As a result, they often eat unhealthful fast foods or processed foods available in local convenience stores.

Community gardens increase food security by promoting consumption of local foods. Studies have shown that community gardens involve community members, including the food-insecure, in the production of fresh, locally grown, healthful food. Community garden founders also hope to build communities and increase members' feelings of self-sufficiency.

The White House serves as an example in the use of community gardens to promote health and food security. First Lady Michelle Obama started a White House garden in 2009. In 2012, discussing her reasons for starting the garden, she said, "We have a wonderful history in this country of community gardening and somehow along the way we lost that tradition. Part of what we hope to see is people reconnecting to that part of our heritage." Improving food security is one of many reasons twenty-first-century citizens are returning to community gardening. Urban gardeners want to grow fresh foods and ensure healthful food sources. Many also see community gardens as a way to live more sustainably. Producing homegrown food decreases the use of industrial chemicals and equipment and the need to transport food. In addition, it saves money on food and provides recreation and exercise.

Physical and Mental Health

In addition to improving nutrition, many studies show that gardening improves mental health. Gardeners share food or flowers with neighbors or give excess food to neighborhood food banks. They meet people through

To Your
HEALTH

MICHELLE OBAMA PROMOTES GARDENS

In 2009, First Lady Michelle Obama, White House staff members, volunteers, and local schoolchildren planted the first White House Kitchen Garden. It was a great success, yielding 740 pounds (336 kg) of produce in 1,100 square feet (102 square meters) of space. Since then, the garden has continued to grow and evolve. Its raised beds are fertilized with organic compost and mulched with straw. It grows vegetables and fruits, from lettuce, kale, and other greens to tomatoes, peppers, squash, beans, peas, figs, and blackberries. There is even a beehive in the garden. Bees help with pollination and provide fresh honey. White House chefs use garden produce in White House meals, including state dinners. Approximately one-third of the harvest is donated to Miriam's Kitchen, a Washington, DC, organization that helps homeless people.

First Lady Michelle Obama helps children plant vegetables in the White House garden each spring.

garden clubs and websites. The growing process gives gardeners a sense of pride and accomplishment. They learn about plants, their requirements, and their place in the ecosystem. Gardening decreases stress and causes feelings of reward, mental clarity, and increased self-esteem.

Gardening also aids physical health in the form of exercise, including walking, bending, stretching, and lifting. Outdoor activity provides an additional benefit: sunshine increases vitamin D levels, which improves immune function and decreases the risk of heart disease and stroke.

Economic Benefits

Community gardens benefit their cities or local areas in many ways. Community gardens are much cheaper to develop than parks. They restore vacant lots and decrease litter. They provide retreats from urban noise and open up opportunities for education, entrepreneurship, and employment. This benefits all members of the community, particularly

To Your HEALTH

FRESH VERSUS CANNED OR FROZEN FOOD

Are fresh fruits and vegetables really healthier than canned or frozen ones? It depends. Fresh-picked fruits and vegetables start with more nutrients, and the best way to ensure the highest possible nutrient content is to eat homegrown food directly from the garden. But unless food is eaten or preserved soon after picking, oxygen in the air begins to break down some nutrients. So-called fresh foods in supermarkets that travel for a week and then sit in bins for days lose many nutrients. If vegetables are canned or frozen immediately after picking, they remain high in nutrient content and do not deteriorate, although water-soluble vitamins B and C may break down in canned foods. However, the salt or sugar often added to canned vegetables and fruits decreases their nutritional value. Shoppers should always check labels to see if (and how much) sugar or salt has been added. Frozen vegetables are high in nutrient quality because they are picked and frozen at their peak of ripeness. They are an excellent alternative during the winter when garden-fresh vegetables are not available. Gardeners who freeze or can their own excess produce have the added advantage of knowing exactly what their preserved food contains.

Bending and weeding are beneficial for one's health.

underserved members including immigrants, students, the less wealthy, and the homeless. All community gardens benefit individuals and families economically. Gardeners save money on fresh produce. According to one study, the savings per gardener per season ranged from $75 to $380.

ROOFTOP GARDENS

By 2015, rooftop farms or vegetable gardens were springing up in cities around the world. They help provide urban dwellers with fresh, homegrown produce, while decreasing fossil fuel use for food transport. The biggest challenge of a rooftop garden is weight, so the gardener must first have an architect or contractor inspect the roof to ensure it can withstand the weight of soil, plants, and structures. Proper design can also lighten the load. Instead of garden soil, using potting mix that contains perlite, a lightweight volcanic rock, which improves airflow and drainage. Use lightweight plant containers of plastic, fiberglass, or canvas. Use Styrofoam peanuts (not rocks) for drainage. Because rooftops are windy, install windbreaks such as trellises. Set up a convenient water source, such as an automatic watering system or a built-in storage container.

Environmental Benefits

Growing even a single plant benefits the environment. Plants take in carbon dioxide during photosynthesis and cleanse the air of many pollutants. All plants release oxygen, which is essential to life for most organisms, including humans. Outdoor plants and mulch hold soil in place. This reduces erosion and keeps soil and sediment out of storm drains, streams, and rivers. Native gardens attract pollinators and other wildlife, helping to preserve natural ecosystems.

Both home and community gardens benefit the global environment. Global warming is driven by the addition of greenhouse gases, such as carbon dioxide, to the atmosphere. A person's carbon footprint is a measure of how much (or how little) carbon from fossil fuels his or her lifestyle adds to the atmosphere every year. Growing, processing, and transporting food all contribute to carbon emissions. Add to this the personal fossil fuel costs associated with driving to the grocery store, cooking, and eating in restaurants. Urban gardening reduces the energy needed to process and transport food, so it reduces the carbon footprint of individuals and communities.

During the one to two weeks most food spends in transit or on store shelves, almost 50 percent of it spoils, so growing locally greatly decreases food waste.

CHALLENGES OF GARDENING

Gardeners must provide plants with their basic requirements—nutrients, water, light, air, and soil. They must also protect plants from pests, weather, and other challenges. Both requirements and challenges vary according to the types of plants grown, but the basic challenges apply to any garden—whether in the backyard, schoolyard, or a vacant lot in the community. These challenges include what to grow, where to grow it, supplying basic requirements, protecting your plants, and handling what you produce.

Maintaining a garden is often harder than getting it started. At first, things are exciting—building the beds, planting the first crop, and so on. But it's a long wait until harvest, and later work, such as watering and weeding, is more tedious. Volunteers lose interest. People go on vacation or get busy doing other things. Animals, insects, or vandals may undo much of your hard work.

In addition, bad weather can wreak havoc on your carefully planned garden, even if you take into account the growing season and hardiness

Gardening requires hard work and patience but is very rewarding.

zone. Knowing what zone you live in will help you prepare your garden for the temperatures in your area. Heavy spring rains can flush out your seeds before they sprout. A strong wind can break or rip out tender plants just as they start to take off. A hot, dry summer can burn up the vegetables you have nurtured before they produce. These things happen to all gardeners. You can plan ahead and know your options. If there is time, you can replant seeds or buy new seedlings and start over. You can water during dry spells. Canvas, plastic tents, or umbrellas can be used to shade plants during the hottest part of the day, or if plants are in pots, simply move them. But sometimes, the only option is to learn from experience and try again next year.

Organic Pest Control

Gardeners quickly realize they must compete with many organisms for the food they grow. Many insects eat leaves, burrow into stems, or gnaw

Case In 🌿 POINT
USDA HARDINESS ZONES

Plant hardiness zones reflect average annual minimum temperatures in a given location. Because temperatures are based on thirty-year averages, the range may not include the lowest temperature reached in that zone. Also, every zone has microclimates, or areas with slight variations too small to appear on the map. Microclimates occur in areas that are more sheltered or more exposed (and therefore cooler or warmer) than average for that area. Hardiness zones are guides, not guarantees. A plant in the right hardiness zone may die during an unseasonably hot summer or cold winter. One in a colder zone may grow quite well if planted in a warm microclimate.

Smaller animals, including rabbits, cats, and dogs, can be discouraged from eating and damaging plants by placing chicken wire or netting over garden beds.

holes in garden vegetables and fruits. Many fungi cause plant diseases that sicken, damage, or destroy crops. Weeds grow faster than garden crops, crowd them out, and steal soil nutrients. In some areas, larger pests such

If left unattended, weeds can take over a garden.

as moles, rabbits, and deer are major problems. Moles burrow through the soil, eating and disturbing roots. Rabbits and deer eat most garden crops. As with fertilizers, pest control can be organic or inorganic.

Many organic methods involve being prepared. For example, fences can help keep deer at bay. Insects and fungi are problems everywhere. In the spring, row covers keep out insects. These light pieces of plastic cover the entire row or bed. To limit fungal diseases, water the soil around the plants instead of the plant leaves. If a plant does get a fungus, pull up the entire plant and throw it in the trash. This prevents the fungus from spreading. Crop rotation, or planting different crops in a given spot each year, improves the soil and prevents pests from becoming established. Buying disease-resistant plants also decreases disease. A plant bought at a garden center will have a tag giving information about its growing needs. This tag will tell you if the plant is disease resistant.

To Your
HEALTH

DEALING WITH POLLUTED GARDEN SOIL

City soil is often contaminated by air, water, and soil pollution from vehicles and industry. For example, soils in Boston, Massachusetts, contain lead-based paint, asbestos, coal ash, and automotive oil, among other dangerous pollutants. This causes problems for gardeners trying to grow uncontaminated foods. If possible, grow plants in raised beds, containers, or roof gardens using clean soil and compost. If you must use urban soil, test soil samples first by either purchasing soil test kits or sending samples to professional labs. Sometimes a city makes compost from autumn leaves and other materials collected from residents. The city may bring loads of this compost to a community garden on request. Besides supplying nutrients, mixing compost into the soil dilutes contaminants, decreasing people's risk of toxic exposure.

In addition to eating insects, chickens help with gardening by eating weeds.

Inspecting your garden daily can stop weed or insect infestations early, before they are well established. Pull weeds when they are small and hoeing will not be necessary. Pick off and kill insects such as caterpillars. Backyard chickens (allowed in some urban areas) are handy: fat, juicy

FREEZE YOUR EXTRA VEGETABLES

You may find yourself with more produce than you know what to do with. You can freeze almost any fruit or vegetable, but methods vary slightly depending on type. These general tips apply in most cases:

- Low-acid foods (such as beans, peas, corn, broccoli, and carrots) freeze well.

- Freeze fruits and vegetables when they are freshest.

- Blanch (dip in boiling water for 30 to 60 seconds) produce first, then dip in cold water and dry.

- Wash and dry strawberries, raspberries, and blueberries. Freeze them in a single layer on a baking sheet, then transfer them to a plastic container.

- Store in heavyweight, airtight containers or freezer bags. Fill bags to the top and squeeze out the air.

- Freeze quickly at 0°F (-18°C) or below.

- You can store fruits for about a year and vegetables for eighteen months.

- Some fruits and vegetables get mushy because ice expands as freezing occurs. Knowing this, use vegetables such as squash in soups or stir-fries. Eat berries before they thaw completely.

caterpillars might gross out gardeners, but chickens love them! A lushly growing, well-mulched garden will attract toads, which also love to eat garden pests. A single toad can eat 10,000 bugs during a three-month growing season. Toads must stay moist, so adding a tiny pool (perhaps a mostly buried shallow plastic container filled with water), with a rock as a resting place, will attract toads to your garden.

Beneficial insects, such as ladybugs, eat harmful insects that chew vegetable leaves. The bacterium *Bacillus thuringiensis*, better known as BT, lives naturally in soil and is also sold as a natural insect control agent. When sprayed on the leaves or stems of infected plants, it kills feeding insects. Insecticidal soaps and oil sprays also kill insects. Both must be sprayed directly on the insects. But they also kill beneficial insects, so they must be sprayed carefully.

Using Pesticides

Inorganic methods, such as pesticides, are poisons that kill pests. They include insecticides, herbicides, and fungicides. Because pesticides are toxic by definition, most gardening experts recommend trying less dangerous nonchemical methods first. Pesticides must be used in the right amount, at the right time, and under the right conditions. The gardener must carefully follow label instructions for proper use. Otherwise, plants may be damaged, pests may not be controlled, and people may suffer negative health effects. Many pests are becoming resistant to pesticides. This means more pesticide is required to get the same toxic effect.

Before using any pesticide, it is essential to identify the specific pest and figure out which pesticide will best control it. Insecticides may be effective only at certain stages of an insect's life cycle (only the larval stage or adult stage, for example). The chosen pesticide should be the least toxic option (posing the least risk to both human health and the environment) and should be used with great care. Pesticides should be used only in extreme cases. Often they are used unnecessarily, in excess, and in cases where nontoxic methods would work better. Prevention by using proper gardening practices is the best approach for pest control.

For new gardeners, challenges are many, but rewards are great. The key to success in gardening is to keep learning and experimenting. Research the plants you want to grow before planting. If you think a plant will grow, try it. If it dies or does not produce well, try to figure out why. Develop friendships with other gardeners and ask for their advice. Above all, keep growing.

Pesticides contribute to soil, air, and water pollution.

GARDENING TRENDS

Most gardeners want to grow good, healthful food, have fun, and feel a sense of accomplishment. Others see gardening as a necessity, or at least an important way to obtain fresh food. Gardening is increasing in the United States, and it continues to evolve as ideas, knowledge, and technology change.

Growth and Evolution of Gardening

According to a 2014 report by the National Gardening Association (NGA), 42 million households, or 35 percent of US households, participate in home or community gardens. Since 2008, the number of community gardeners increased by 200 percent. The NGA sees several reasons for the rise in gardening. One is First Lady Michelle Obama's launch of the White House Kitchen Garden and the Let's Move Campaign, initiatives to fight childhood obesity through exercise. Together, the two projects were designed to improve the health of US children by encouraging healthful eating and exercise. Another reason is that government agencies, including the

One urban gardening trend is vertical gardens, which are designed so plants grow on a vertical rather than horizontal surface, making use of limited space.

VERTICAL GARDENS

Vertical gardens may be the ultimate in space-saving greenery. They can attach to any vertical surface—the wall of a house or garage or even a bare fence. The vertical surface must be able to support the weight of the soil and plants. Similar to container gardens, vertical gardens can be made of almost any object that holds soil and water. One type is the pocket, a 15-by-24-inch (38 by 61 cm) container made of breathable, recycled material that is similar to felt and can be attached to any vertical surface. Others include plastic trays divided into individual planting cells, which can be mounted to a surface at an angle, or individual pots clamped to a wall or fence. Even rain gutters and burlap bags can be used for vertical gardens.

USDA and the Department of Health and Human Services, have worked to educate the public about gardening. Finally, partnerships between private organizations, such as the NGA, and federal agencies, such as the USDA, have increased the number of community gardens.

A 2009 survey of gardeners from eight countries suggests that gardeners hope for future developments in technology that would lead to gardens that can water and feed themselves, and that would enable gardeners to simulate different soil and weather conditions. Such technologies would help gardeners grow plants, such as tropical plants, that previously grew only in their natural habitats or in greenhouses. The survey also suggests a likely increase in use of green roofs, vertical gardens, and rainwater recovery systems, such as rain gardens (designed to control

KEYHOLE GARDENS

Keyhole gardens began in Africa, but they are now becoming popular in hot, dry regions of the United States. A keyhole garden is circular, with a notch cut into one side. From above, the garden looks like a keyhole. In the center is a compost pile made from kitchen and garden waste and household wastewater. The compost pile holds heat, moisture, and nutrients, and it nourishes the surrounding garden. The notch provides easy access to the compost pile, which may be held in place with rocks or built up inside a chicken-wire enclosure. Vegetables are grown around the rest of the circle, which is usually lined with rocks or bricks to hold in the soil.

runoff), which are already in use. Overall, gardeners expect future garden technology to be more intelligent, or computer-controlled, and at the same time more organic, or environmentally sound. Gardeners will likely develop more self-sufficient lifestyles, producing more of their own food, as they replace typical lawns with yards that provide food as well as grass. In the meantime, certain gardening trends are already on the rise.

The Rise of Rainscaping

The Philadelphia Horticultural Society foresees a rise in natural watering systems. Rainscaping is the process of using rainwater more efficiently. It addresses both flooding and drought, which will likely continue to increase in the near future due to climate change. One example of rainscaping is a rain garden. Rain gardens exist throughout the country. They are usually associated with wetter locations, in cities or suburbs where storm water runoff is a problem. They can be designed and built by individual families or neighborhoods, or in common areas such as schools or parks. Rain gardens are shallow, depressed areas planted with perennials (for example common rush, butterfly weed, or cardinal flower) to capture and hold large amounts of rainwater. In addition, they absorb and filter storm water. Soil under the garden may be specially engineered to capture and hold water and slow down runoff. Both plants and soil absorb excess nutrients. Excess water drains into storm sewers.

Oyas are another method of rainscaping. They are often used in drought-prone areas, such as the desert Southwest. Their function is not necessarily to trap rainwater, but to provide constant moisture to plant roots and thus reduce water waste. These large, rounded terra-cotta pots

Rain gardens can be beautiful, and because of the types of plants they contain, they often attract butterflies and hummingbirds.

with narrow openings are buried in a raised bed or other planting area. In the absence of rain, the gardener fills them with water every seven to ten days. Water gradually leaks through the porous terra-cotta and into the garden. Plants grow toward the moist area. Both rain gardens and oyas work with nature to conserve water. They use simple technology to achieve both beauty and sustainability.

Mobile Gardening

One meaning of the term *mobile gardening* is the simple idea that gardens can be planted even where good soil is not available. Mobile gardening is becoming increasingly popular. Many modern gardens are located in cities or suburbs, where the ground is mostly concrete or the soil is poor or contaminated. In these areas, raised beds and container gardens can be substituted for in-ground gardens. Gardening supply companies now sell raised bed kits in different sizes, which gardeners assemble and fill with soil of their choosing. Some kits are hard plastic and snap together. Others are wooden planks that fit together with screw-on brackets. Many mobile

Case In POINT

THE BICYCLE GARDEN

A novel type of mobile garden is the bicycle garden. People are putting tiny herb or flower gardens in bicycle baskets or attaching plant containers elsewhere on bikes. One bike gardener attached a sign to the bike, telling passersby to help themselves to salad greens. Another wrapped parts of her bike in cheesecloth and burlap and added sprouting seeds, such as wheat or barley. Many people use retired bikes as stationary planters or garden art. Wrapping the frame in sphagnum moss, for example, allows plants to grow over the entire bicycle.

Mobile gardens, such as bicycle gardens, can be easily moved from place to place.

gardens are fitted with wheels and can be rolled across a deck or patio and placed wherever the gardener wishes. Some are also elevated and fitted with automatic watering devices.

Another very different meaning of mobile gardening relates to the growing variety of gardening apps for mobile phones and tablet computers. These programs provide instant information on a variety of gardening topics. For example, the free app Garden Compass provides information on a plant's blooming season and how much light the plant needs. Or a gardener can photograph an unidentified plant or pest, send the photo to the Garden Compass team, and have an expert answer a question. The app Garden Time Planner tells users whether to grow a vegetable, herb, or flower from seeds indoors or directly in the garden. It includes a checklist of steps to take throughout the year, videos with planting instructions, and a weather report.

Pollinator Gardens

Pollination is the transfer of pollen from the anthers (male structures) of one flower to the stigma (female structure) of another flower. This process leads to fertilization, or sexual reproduction, and it is necessary for seeds and fruits to develop. Agriculture, which includes gardening, depends on pollination. Sometimes pollination occurs by wind, but approximately 75 percent of the world's flowering plants rely on animal pollinators, mostly insects, birds, and bats.

In the United States, honeybees and native pollinators are declining. Reasons for pollinator decline include loss of habitat, high levels of pesticides in the environment, and parasites, including mites, introduced from abroad. This decline affects both the types and prices of food we eat. As gardeners become aware of this situation, they are beginning to develop

Pollinator gardens can be designed to attract a specific type of pollinator, such as bees or butterflies.

gardens designed to attract pollinators by providing pollinator habitats and food sources.

Pollinator gardens benefit the major organisms that pollinate our fruit and vegetable crops—bees, wasps, butterflies, hummingbirds, and bats. Each pollinator prefers flowers of varying size, color, scent, and design. Many garden vegetables require pollinators, and often gardeners mix ornamental flowers, such as lilies and sunflowers, with their vegetables to tempt more pollinators. Native plants are most attractive to pollinators

Types and styles of gardens are ever-expanding.

and provide the best food sources because the plants and pollinators have coevolved and depend on each other.

Recent trends and developments in gardening—including rainscaping, mobile gardens, and pollinator gardens—can be used by gardeners of all ages, in any type of garden. They can be adapted to fit backyards, community gardens, patios, or rooftops. When properly designed, they grow well in either wet or dry areas. Gardeners are seeking ways to combine new technology and techniques to make gardening easier and more enjoyable. At the same time, they want to grow healthful food and contribute to a sustainable environment.

Working as a
COMMUNITY FARM DIRECTOR

J osh Slotnick is cofounder and director of the Program in Ecological Agriculture and Society (PEAS) Farm in Missoula, Montana. PEAS Farm began in 1996 to supply food to the Missoula Food Bank and to the WIC Program for low-income women, infants, and children. It began with thirty University of Montana students, who learned about sustainable farming through hands-on training while producing food. Under Slotnick's direction, the students raised $50,000; built fences, sheds, and a greenhouse; and developed a 6.5-acre (2.6 hectare) garden.

Slotnick oversees the student farm. The program schedules and runs field trips, conducts summer camps, and helps organize school gardens and after-school programs.

"I work all the time," Slotnick says. But no two days are the same. In February, everyone works in the greenhouse, making potting soil, filling trays, and sowing seeds. Later, they spread compost, till the compost in, and prepare growing beds. When the soil is warm enough, they transplant the greenhouse seedlings and vegetables such as peas, beans, and corn. Then they move irrigation pipe to deliver water to the new plants. As the plants start receiving water, their growth takes off, and the big challenge is keeping the weeds at bay.

Although Slotnick is the farm director and does the paperwork, communication, and other tasks associated with a director's job, he also works side by side with the students and other young gardeners every day. Slotnick says, "When you weed the carrots, they grow beautifully, and you bring them to the food bank, and you see that you've been personally effective. You realize that you can actually make a change in the world."

GLOSSARY

artificial: not natural; made by people rather than nature

compost: a common type of organic fertilizer made from decaying organic matter such as dead leaves, garden and food waste, and manure; a natural (nonartificial) type of fertilizer

homesteading: originally, living and working on free land provided by the federal government; more recently, returning to the land to live a more self-sufficient lifestyle

native garden: a garden containing local plants that have adapted well to the area

rainscaping: gardening techniques that use water more efficiently to lessen the effect of floods and droughts

sustainability: living in a way that preserves and maintains the ability of the environment to survive and continuously produce its resources without being used up or destroyed

till: to turn over and dig up soil, using a tiller, plow, or hand implement

SOURCE NOTES

18. Heidi Godman, "Backyard Gardening: Grow Your Own Food, Improve Your Health," *Harvard Health Publications* (2012), http://www.health.harvard.edu/blog/backyard-gardening-grow-your-own-food-improve-your-health-201206294984.

31. "The First Lady Cultivates 'American Grown' Gardening," *NPR Books*, May 29, 2012, http://www.npr.org/2012/05/29/153705721/the-first-lady-cultivates-american-grown-gardening.

60. Jeremy N. Smith, *The Urban Garden: How One Community Turned Idle Land into a Garden City and How You Can, Too* (New York: Skyhorse Publishing, 2014), 14.

SELECTED BIBLIOGRAPHY

"Benefits of Organic Gardening," *Organic Gardening 101*, 2009. http://www.organicgardening-101.com/benefits-of-organic-gardening.html.

"Community Gardens: Potential Challenges," *City of Redwood City*, 2012. http://www.redwoodcity.org/manager/initiatives/gardens/challenges.html.

Darnton, Julia and Lauren McGuire, "What Are the Physical and Mental Benefits of Gardening?" *Michigan State University Extension*, May 19, 2014. http://msue.anr.msu.edu/news/what_are_the_physical_and_mental_benefits_of_gardening.

"How to Plan a Vegetable Garden," *Better Homes & Gardens*, 2015. http://www.bhg.com/gardening/vegetable/vegetables/planning-your-first-vegetable-garden/.

Joy, LaManda. *Start a Community Food Garden: The Essential Handbook*, London: Timber Press, 2014.

"Multiple Benefits of Community Gardening," *Gardening Matters*, 2012. http://www.gardeningmatters.org/sites/default/files/Multiple%20Benefits_2012.pdf.

Pleasant, Barbara, "Top Gardening Challenges and How to Overcome Them," *Mother Earth News*, 2014. http://www.motherearthnews.com/organic-gardening/organic-vegetable-gardening-challenges-zm0z14amzsto.aspx.

Smith, Jeremy N. *The Urban Garden: How One Community Turned Idle Land into a Garden City and How You Can, Too*. New York: Skyhorse Publishing, 2014.

"Why Garden? The National Garden Bureau's Top Ten," *National Garden Bureau, Inc.*, 2006. http://ngb.org/todays_garden/index.cfm.

FURTHER INFORMATION

Akeroyd, Simon. *Kitchen Gardening for Beginners*. New York: DK Publishing, 2013. Read about simple gardening guidelines for growing vegetables and fruits in your own kitchen.

The American Community Gardening Association
http://communitygarden.org
Check out and download their course on environmental education in community gardens.

Green, Jen. *A Teen Guide to Eco-Gardening, Food, and Cooking*. Chicago: Capstone Heinemann, 2013. After growing your own fruits and vegetables, learn about how to prepare and cook them!

Madigan, Carleen. *The Backyard Homestead*. North Adams, MA: Storey Publishing, 2009. Learn how to transform your backyard into a garden.

My First Garden
http://urbanext.illinois.edu/firstgarden
Learn how to plan for your own beginner garden.

National Gardening Association
http://www.garden.org/home
This nonprofit organization has resources and information on gardening for kids, including school gardens.

Perdew, Laura. *Eating Local*. Minneapolis, MN: Lerner, 2016. Read about the ways in which you can eat local, and why it's important to do so.

Trail, Gayla. *Grow Great Grub: Organic Food from Small Spaces*. New York: Clarkson Potter, 2010. Read about how to turn even the smallest spaces, such as your kitchen windowsill, into a garden.

INDEX

backyard gardens, 16, 19

canning, 9, 10

community gardens, 7, 14, 21–23, 30–32, 34–35, 36, 43, 48, 50, 59

companion planting, 7, 16

compost, 16, 19, 21, 25–27, 32, 43, 51

container gardens, 16, 50, 54

farmers' markets, 4

fertilizers, 8, 10, 12, 16, 24–27, 32, 42

food security, 31

gardening benefits, 28–37

gardening challenges, 38–47

in-ground gardens, 19, 54

keyhole gardens, 51

kitchen gardens, 18, 32, 48

kitchen scrap gardening, 30

mobile gardens, 54–56, 59

Obama, Michelle, 31, 32, 48

organic gardens, 16, 26

pest control, 43–47

pesticides, 10, 12, 16, 28, 46–47, 56

pollinator gardens, 56–59

pollution, 12, 14, 43

rain gardens, 50–54

raised-bed gardens, 4, 18, 19–21, 32, 43, 53, 54

rooftop gardens, 36, 43, 59

root crops, 9

square-foot gardens, 20–21

three sisters gardens, 7, 8

urban gardens, 12, 14–15, 32, 37

vertical gardens, 50

White House Kitchen Garden, 31, 32, 48

Photo Acknowledgments

The images in this book are used with the permission of: © Albachiaraa/Shutterstock Images, p. 1; © Seiya Kawamoto/Digital Vision/Thinkstock, p. 5; © LisaInGlasses/iStockphoto, p. 6; © YinYang/iStockphoto, p. 9; © Neveshkin Nikolay/Shutterstock Images, p. 10; © Ungnoikalookjeab/iStockphoto/Thinkstock, p. 11; © Morley/US Government Printing Office, p. 13; © Mike Harrington/Getty Images, p. 14; © Jenny Sturm/Shutterstock Images, p. 17; © mtreasure/iStockphoto, p. 19; © Skystorm/iStockphoto, p. 20; © Laura Stone/Shutterstock Images, p. 22; © Janine Lamontagne/iStockphoto, p. 25; © Valentina Razumova/Shutterstock Images, p. 26; © Susan Chiang/iStockphoto, p. 29; © Bao Dandan Xinhua News Agency/Newscom, p. 33; © Innershadows Photography/Shutterstock Images, p. 35; © ChameleonsEye/Shutterstock Images, p. 37; © XiXinXing/Shutterstock Images, p. 39; © Martin Meehan/iStockphoto, p. 41; © Oleksandr Shevchenko/Shutterstock Images, p. 42; © Nastya Glazneva/Shutterstock Images, p. 44; © LDprod/Shutterstock Images, p. 47; © smuay/Shutterstock Images, p. 49; © David Snyder/ZumaPress/Corbis, p. 51; © Yangchao/Shutterstock Images, p. 53; © Piotr Wawrzyniuk/Shutterstock Images, p. 55; © Trofimov Denis/Shutterstock Images, p. 57; © Dean Hoffmeyer/Richmond Times-Dispatch/AP Images, p. 58.

Front Cover: © Zygotehaasnobrain/Shutterstock.com (top left); © iStockphoto.com/JBryson (top right); © John Lee/Blend Images/Getty Images (bottom left); © Albachiaraa/Shutterstock.com (bottom right).

The
Boys who Saved
The Children

Margaret Baldwin

JULIAN MESSNER · NEW YORK

A JEM BOOK

Published by Julian Messner, a Simon & Schuster
Division of Gulf & Western Corporation,
Simon & Schuster Building,
1230 Avenue of the Americas,
New York, New York 10020.
JULIAN MESSNER and colophon are trademarks of
Simon & Schuster, registered in the U.S. Patent
and Trademark Office.

Manufactured in the United States of America.

Design by Regine deToledo

Pictures courtesy of YIVO Institute for Jewish Research

Library of Congress Cataloging in Publication Data

Baldwin, Margaret, 1948-
    The boys who saved the children.

    "A Jem book."
    Adaptation of: Growing up in the Holocaust / Ben
Edelbaum.
    Summary: Ben Edelbaum describes the courage
and strength which held his family together
during the terror of the years in the Lodz ghetto
until they were separated in Auschwitz.
    1. Holocaust, Jewish (1939-1945)—Poland—Lodz
—Personal narratives—Juvenile literature.
    2. Edelbaum, Ben, 1928-   —Juvenile literature.
    3. Jews—Poland—Lodz—Persecutions—Juvenile
literature.   4. Lodz (Poland)—Ethnic relations
—Juvenile literature.   [1. Holocaust, Jewish
(1939-1945)—Poland—Lodz—Personal narratives.
    2. Edelbaum, Ben, 1928-   ]   I. Edelbaum,
Ben, 1928-   . Growing up in the Holocaust.
II. Title.
D810.J4B287   940.53'15'03924   81-14084
ISBN 0-671-43603-1   AACR2

This story is adapted from a remarkable book, *Growing up in the Holocaust*. It was written and published by Ben Edelbaum. This story is true. It is one of many moving accounts in the book of the courage and strength that held one family together. The time was during the terror of the years in the Lodz Ghetto, until they were finally separated, some forever, at Auschwitz.

This book is dedicated to Ben and Dora Edelbaum, two people who have become very special to me. They have taught me a great deal. It is also dedicated to all those who, like Ben and Dora, survived the Holocaust and brought their stories to the world. They are a constant reminder not only of the horror man can inflict upon his fellow man, but of the triumph of the human spirit over the worst horror.

IN 1940 THE GERMAN NAZIS ROUNDED UP over 270,000 Polish Jews. They herded them into a section of the city of Lodz, Poland. They then sealed this area off from contact with the outside world. It became known as the Lodz Ghetto. Ben Edelbaum and his family survived in this ghetto for four years. Conditions were brutal. The Germans were determined to break the spirit of these people. Already they were destroying them in the death camps. Food in the ghetto was scarce. Ben once saw a young man kill a woman for a loaf of bread. The Germans did not let the people have enough coal to heat the crowded apartment buildings. It was so cold one winter that ice formed on the walls inside Ben's room.

The Jews — men, women, and children — were forced to work long hours for the Nazis. They worked in factories to help the war effort. Only those who could work, and were therefore useful to the Nazis, were allowed to live. The very young, the very old, the weak, and the sick were hauled off to death camps.

CHAPTER
ONE

I CANNOT TELL YOU THE HORROR OF AN Aktion. This means "action" in German. It was the term used by the Nazis when their soldiers came into the ghetto to take away those they felt had no right to live, those who were unfit. Already my older sister, Esther, had been taken. I remember my last sight of her. She stood in a truck in her nightgown with the other hospital patients, afraid, confused. Then the truck drove away. At least she did not see the soldiers throw her newly born infant daughter to her death from the hospital window.

The Nazis would come for us in the night or the early morning. It was always the same. We awoke to sounds of screams and shouts. People ran in panic from street to street, trying to escape. Of course, there was no escape. Little children were dragged from their mothers' arms. Husbands were taken from their wives. Grandparents were torn from their families. Sometimes we heard shots. Maybe the Nazis had caught someone trying to hide. Maybe someone did not obey a command fast enough.

And now, once more, rumors of an *Aktion* had started. Rumors in the ghetto nearly always came true. We had no reason to doubt

this one. And it began. The soldiers moved from street to street. They came closer each day. The day before, they had been in the street next to ours. The next morning, they would come for us.

That night, families from the other apartments in our building gathered in our room. We talked about the coming horror.

"I know they will take him," Rachel whispered. Tears flowed from her eyes. She was looking at her little son, Herschel. The child was six, but he could not walk. He had to be pushed around in a cart.

None of us said anything. What could we say? We knew Rachel was right. Herschel was just the type of person the Germans got rid of. He was a child and useless and a cripple. He had no right to live. But he was all Rachel had left in the world. Her young husband had been one of the first to disappear.

"There must be somewhere to hide him!" my father stated.

"Under the bed?" my sister suggested.

"In the closet?" my other sister asked.

"No," my father shook his head. "Those are the first places the soldiers search when they come into the apartment."

"Then we'll hide him in the open," my

mother said firmly.

We all stared at her. No one spoke. We were all thinking the same thing. My mother was very frail and weak. We were certain that she was in as much danger of being taken away as little Herschel.

My mother walked over and picked up one of the huge sacks the Germans used to give us our skimpy ration of potatoes.

"Get inside," she told little Herschel.

The boy went inside the potato sack without question. Although he was only six, he had been forced to grow up fast. We all had.

"Now," said my mother, "when the Germans come, you must lie very still and not make a sound. Can you do that?"

"Yes," Herschel answered from inside the potato sack.

My mother dragged the sack with Herschel in it near the stove. She draped it to look as if it had just been dumped there. It was perfect. Herschel was just another sack of potatoes!

That cheered everyone up. They began to talk more happily, mostly about food. Food had become the most important thing in our lives. But I soon grew tired of hearing about the different kinds of potatoes everyone had.

How many were frozen or rotten. How many each person got. How they cooked them. Sam and Rita, our neighbors across the hall, came over. I left. I went over to their apartment to spend the evening with Sala.

Sala was near my age. Both of us were about thirteen. She was my closest friend. We had known each other for over a year. We walked to work together, unless she was working the night shift. We waited in food lines together, often for hours. Sometimes I carried her packages for her. That was dangerous in the ghetto. A person who offered to carry your food might run off with it! She trusted me.

Hunger pains often kept us from sleeping. Sala and I spent the long evenings trying to keep our minds off food. We talked about the happy times we had known as children. I showed her the diary I was keeping. She showed me her stamp collection. She had a beautiful singing voice. She sang the sad ghetto songs of our people until tears came to my eyes.

That night, she was terribly frightened.

"Oh, Ben," she said as she saw me, "I know they will take little Herschel. And me!"

She began to cry.

I felt very helpless.

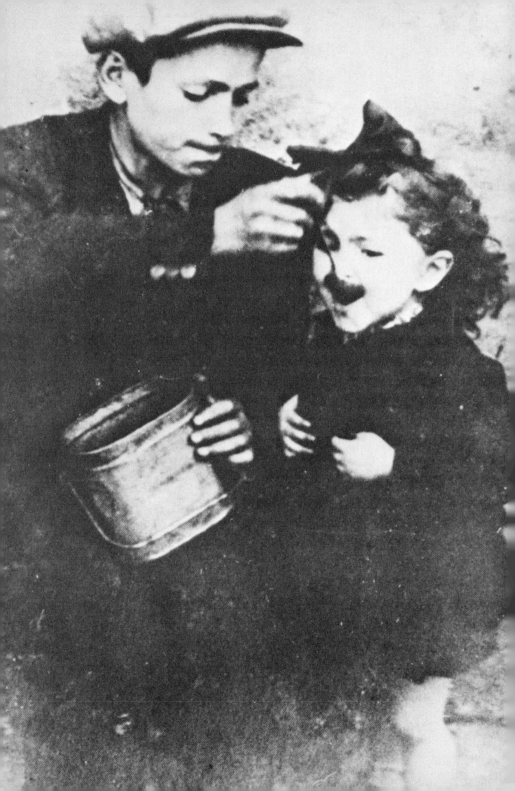

"But if they take you," she wept, "I want to go too."

I walked over to her and took her in my arms. I had never held her before. We sat there, holding onto each other. Then, to my surprise, I kissed her. Through her tears, she kissed me back. I found myself wondering if I would live to be a man. Would I love and marry a woman like Sala?

"Why did this have to happen to us?" Sala cried. "Why were we born now?"

I had no answer. Being together seemed to comfort both of us. Sala stopped crying. She was even able to smile when I had to go.

I returned home. The neighbors had gone.

We all sat quietly, thinking about the terror of the coming morning.

Finally my mother spoke.

"If they take me," she said calmly, "I don't want you to cry and show you are upset. It might make them angry. They might do someone else harm. Just take my food ration and do not grieve for me."

"I won't have you talking that way!" my father shouted angrily. We stared at him, amazed. I had never heard my gentle father raise his voice in anger to anyone, especially not to my mother.

He broke down and began to weep. We all did, holding onto each other. We were so tired of the hunger, the cold, the fear.

"Come on, stop this," my sister said. "We better go to bed. We need to look well rested in the morning."

She meant that as a joke, but no one laughed. A good night's sleep and the healthy look it brought could mean the difference between life and death.

CHAPTER
TWO

THEY CAME AT 6:00 A.M.

We heard the screams and shouts. We heard the sound of running feet.

"They're here," someone yelled. "They have already shot a woman. She did not move fast enough when they said to leave the building. They thought she was trying to hide."

My sisters quickly took some beet juice. They dabbed it on my mother's cheeks and lips to make her look more healthy.

Rachel came in with little Herschel. Hurriedly, we put him in the sack.

"Now, my child," she said. She was trying to keep from crying. "The soldiers will come into the room. You must not move or cry out for me. Do you understand?"

"Yes, Mama." Little Herschel was so scared I doubted if he could have made a sound anyway. We closed the sack and left him.

"Everyone out!" came the shouts from the streets. I looked out of my window to see the Nazi soldiers. They had guns in their hands as they walked down the street.

My father began to pray. I wanted to, but the words wouldn't come out aloud. I said them over and over in my heart. We crowded out into the hall. Sala found me. I took her

hand and we held each other tightly all the way down the stairs.

Once in the street, though, Sala and I were torn apart. She was made to stand with her family and I with mine.

We waited while the soldiers went up and searched each apartment. I looked at Rachel. She was white with fear. She had no way of knowing if they had found Herschel and killed him. She could do nothing but stand and wait.

Ten minutes passed.

Finally the Nazis came out. They moved through the crowd, looking at each of us. My heart nearly stopped beating as they came to our family. Their cold eyes swept over us. They passed on.

But when they reached Sala's family, they grabbed Sala and dragged her to the waiting truck. My throat hurt. My heart raced in hatred and anger, but there was nothing I could do. I saw Sam, her father, holding onto her mother. She was close to fainting. The soldiers took two little brothers from their parents, and an elderly woman. Then they left, moving on to the next building. We stood in the street awaiting orders.

The truck drove off. Sala leaned out the back.

"I love you!" she shouted over and over again. "I love you!"

Tears ran down my cheeks into my mouth. I knew she was talking to her parents, but I hoped a little of that love was meant for me.

Finally we were told to return to our homes. The morning work shift was due to report to the factories soon.

Rachel ran up the stairs in a panic. She tore open the potato sack. There sat little Herschel, scared and cramped, but safe!

Until the next time....

CHAPTER
THREE

OUR BLEAK LIVES WENT ON.

Before the war my father had made fur coats. Now he, my uncle, and I all worked in a factory making fur coats for the Germans. When they had forced us to leave our homes, the Nazis had taken all our possessions. They took furniture, money, and clothing, and stored them in warehouses. Our job in the factory was to make new fur coats out of the ones they had stolen from us.

I was foreman in charge of a work group of twelve boys, all about my age. We worked ten hours a day. We had nothing to eat except a bowl of hot broth and coffee. But we boys were very proud of the fact that we were doing grown-up work. It ensured our right to live.

Our job was to cut the fur coats apart and rip out the linings. We had to finish an exact number of coats per day. I got very good at it. I could rip up a coat without damaging the fur in six to eight minutes. I would lay it out, ready to be resewn.

Then, one day, our jobs changed. All the men, women, and children were put to work making white sheepskin coats for the Nazi soldiers fighting on the Russian front.

These coats were very hard to make. Sheepskin is oily. The fur is thick and rough

and clumps together. The Germans used sheepskin because it kept out the snow and the bitter cold. To this day, my thumbs are bent out of shape from pushing the fur back from underneath the sewing machines.

We made hundreds of these coats and shipped them out daily. My boys and I kept up the same pace as the grown-ups. We were very proud of this. We kept telling ourselves that the Nazis must be proud of us too.

Then the white coats began coming back—for repairs.

They were mostly damaged in the same way. There were holes in the front of the coat and even bigger holes in the back. Stained with blood, the holes showed where the bullets had hit. At first there were only a few coats. Then there were more and more. Finally we were working on repairs all the time. We had no news, of course. However, from these coats we could tell that the war was not going well for the Nazis in Russia.

We were ordered to go through the pockets of the coats. We had to bring anything we found to our factory supervisor. We found very little, usually cigarette tobacco. Once, however, we found an arm in a coat sleeve. It had been severed from the body. We

were terribly upset and so was our supervisor. He told the Germans. They came and wrapped it in a blanket in a very solemn ceremony. It was taken away and, we heard, given a military burial. Not long after this, I found a note in the pocket of the coat I was working on.

"May the new wearer of this coat find better luck," it read.

The factory supervisor, Mr Blaugrund, was a very kind man. He did not use his position of authority to take advantage of us, as some did in the ghetto. Instead, he tried to help us. He made our lives as comfortable as it was in his power to do. We thought a great deal of him in return. We did not hesitate to bring our problems to him.

One day, his beloved wife died.

The Nazis had strictly forbidden any type of religious services for us in the ghetto. But every day, after the death of Mr. Blaugrund's wife, we met in secret in his office. He hung a sign on the door that read, "Conference." And every day we said the ritual prayers for the dead for his wife. If the Nazis had caught us, I am sure every one of us would have been shot.

Soon after that, the dreadful rumors started again.

There was going to be another *Aktion*. This time they were going to take all the children.

CHAPTER
FOUR

As I have said, rumors in the ghetto nearly always came true. They were passed along by those who worked closely with the Germans. Perhaps it was someone in the special Jewish police force that worked in the ghetto who had overheard an officer talking. Soon everyone knew about it. All the children would be taken away. We had little doubt about where they would take us.

My boys and I talked about it as we worked. It was not fair, we decided. At fourteen, I worked next to two grown-up men and kept up with them easily. In fact, I could sometimes do the work better. I was stronger and quicker. Lack of food had not been as hard on me as on the older men.

We knew we had to do something to prove to the Germans we had the right to stay alive. We thought and thought. There was no use in showing them our work. The Nazis would never come to the factory. Even if they did, they would not have been interested. We had to do something to catch their attention.

But what?

The rumors got louder. It was only a matter of time, they said. They would not leave one child in the ghetto.

Every day we talked over different plans.

None seemed any good. We were getting desperate. Then one day one of the boys heard something. The wife of the German officer in charge was going to have a birthday in a few weeks.

"That's it," I cried. "We will give her a present. Something we have made ourselves. Something to show we are hardworking and can do the work of adults. We will make her a fur coat!"

We talked it over. It seemed the only way left to us to escape death. It would be hard. We had just a few short weeks. But at least it gave us hope. It gave us something to do to try to save ourselves.

We went to Mr. Blaugrund and explained our plan. He agreed that it was a good idea. He promised to get permission from the Nazis to use some of the fur in the warehouse to make the coat. Since the coat was not for ourselves, but for a German, the Nazis granted us permission.

We decided to make a Persian paw fur coat. We got Frau Biebow's measurements and began working immediately. We did not have much time.

A Persian lamb coat is made from the fur of the lamb's paws, the most beautiful part.

The fur is short and curly and makes a lovely, swirled pattern. But it only comes in small pieces, no bigger than a lamb's paw. Each piece is about six inches long and two inches wide. These pieces were sewn together by hand to make long panels. There were maybe twenty or thirty pieces per panel. Then the panels were sewn together, again by hand, to make the coat. After that, the lining for the coat had to be made. It was a lot of work. However, we were set on doing it all ourselves. Our fathers gave us advice, now and then, but that was all.

Of course, we had to keep up with our daily work too. We put in our ten-hour shift. Then we worked overtime for several hours. We even took the pieces of fur home at night.

The skin on the fur was very thin and brittle. All the sewing had to be done with tiny, fine needles. If not, the delicate skin would break. It took hour after hour. I often worked by candlelight at night. The Nazis turned off all the electricity at 8:00 P.M. I stitched and stitched, taking tiny stitches until I thought I would go blind. My hands and fingers ached from holding the thin needles.

But at least I was doing something.

The small patches of fur were sewn into

the panels. Then we began to sew the long panels together. This, too, was done with the same tiny stitches. We worked and worked.

All the time the rumors got louder and louder.

We were running out of time.

CHAPTER
FIVE

The day of Frau Biebow's birthday drew closer. It seemed we would never be finished in time. We began work on the lining of the coat. Our fathers stopped us just as we were about to cut it out. We had come close to making a terrible mistake. We were going to cut the lining smaller than the coat. This seemed logical since the lining would fit inside the coat. But that was not right, our fathers said. The lining must be larger so that it would not bind and pull. It must stretch or the fur part would crease around it.

We cut and sewed for our very lives.

Finally the coat was finished. It was the day before Frau Biebow's birthday. Everyone in the factory, from Mr. Blaugrund on down, gathered to admire it. It was truly a beautiful coat. The panels of lamb's fur swirled in lovely designs. It had to be a beautiful coat. The lives of hundreds of children, we believed, depended on it. It was full-length, with long sleeves and fancy buttons. The buttons were taken from the coats of our people that were stacked in the warehouse. We brushed the coat carefully. Then we folded it up, and put it in a box. But it was not packed until every boy who had worked on it had hung a tag on the bottom of each panel he had sewn. On that tag

were his name, address—and age.

Now, how to deliver it?

This would not be easy. The Nazi High Command was locked away from us in an office building outside the ghetto walls. One had to have a written pass to get by the Jewish police on our side. Then one had to pass the German soldiers on their side.

Mr. Blaugrund agreed to help.

He took me up to his office. His secretary telephoned the central command building. She asked for Commandant Biebow's secretary. We waited. She answered the phone. Mr. Blaugrund motioned for me to pick up the receiver.

My voice shook.

"This is Ben Edelbaum," I said. "Several of us have made a present for Frau Biebow's birthday. I need permission to deliver it to her. May I bring it over today?"

There was silence. I suppose the secretary had to go and get permission from someone else. Finally she came back to the phone and asked to speak to Mr. Blaugrund.

It was all arranged.

Mr. Blaugrund's secretary wrote a pass for me. As foreman, I had been chosen to deliver the coat.

I took the box. Everyone watched me leave.

I walked through the ghetto. Everywhere I went, I seemed to see the children. I saw them waiting in the food lines for hours, for the little bit of food we had to live on. I saw them trudging to work in the factories, day and night shifts, ten hours at a stretch. All of us doing exactly the same work as the adults. I saw the children, their faces pinched with hunger. I saw them and I thought of what we should be doing. Laughing, playing, going to school. I thought of Sala. I knew I would never see her again.

Not one child I passed looked at me and smiled. We had forgotten how to smile, how to laugh. We lived in fear. Fear of not meeting our share of the work load. Fear of having nothing at all to eat tomorrow. Fear of the *Aktion* and the death camps.

As I walked along, I had the strangest feeling that I held the lives of these children in my hands. There was a kind of horror in the thought that the lives of hundreds were sewn up in a Persian fur coat—a gift for the wife of a German officer, made from the fur they had stolen from us.

I arrived at the central command build-

ing. My box and my pass were clutched tightly in my shaking hands.

I could see nothing but walls and barbed wire and closed gates. The Jewish police looked very stern and frightening. And beyond them were the Nazi soldiers.

My courage very nearly gave out. Then I thought of all the long nights of work. I thought of all the children I had seen. I thought of my friends. I thought of Sala.

I handed the man my pass.

CHAPTER
SIX

THE JEWISH POLICE GAVE MY PASS AND ME a casual glance. Then they called through the gate to the Germans on the other side. These men had developed a friendship of sorts from working together day after day. The Germans waved me through. I was past the first barrier.

I waited.

Soon a woman in a uniform and high, dark boots came up to me.

"Are you Edelbaum?" she asked.

"Yes, ma'am," I replied.

"Follow me." She walked into the building. I followed, the coatbox in my hand.

"Sit here," she ordered. I sat on a bench in front of a room marked Number 3 on the door. I sat for a long time. People came and went. They all looked so healthy and well fed! Their clothes were clean and pressed.

I had put on my best clothes that day. They were little more than rags, although my mother did her best to keep them mended and clean. I felt like a beggar. And, indeed, I was a beggar. I was a child come to beg for the lives of other children. Only that morning we had heard that the soldiers would be coming for us any day.

Suddenly the door to Room Number 3 opened. Someone came out, I think, but I did not really notice. Because there, just opposite me, was a picture of Adolf Hitler.

I froze in terror.

I cannot explain the effect the picture of this man had on me. He was the cause of the fear and misery we lived in every day. He was set upon getting rid of us, wiping out our entire race. We had all heard rumors of the death camps, where hundreds, maybe thousands of Jews, died daily. Hitler was just a man, we told ourselves. He was a person like any of us. But in our hearts he had become an evil superman. His picture alone came to represent death and terror. And so the sight of his face pinned me to the bench as surely as if he had run a knife through me.

I longed to run away. But I could not move. The picture stared down at me.

A woman came up and stood in front of me. It was the woman in the boots and uniform. For a moment I was afraid she had come to take me into that room. To him!

I shook with fear.

"Is that it?" she asked, pointing at the box.

I could only nod yes.

"I will see Frau Biebow gets it," she said.

She picked up the box and walked away.

Not knowing what else to do, I stood up, turned around, and ran out of that building. Once outside the gate, I felt as though I had been let out of jail. I did not stop running until I had run all the way through the ghetto streets back to the factory.

All the boys were still there.

I had nothing to tell them.

We began to wait.

CHAPTER
SEVEN

Four days passed.

We heard nothing.

Our hearts sank.

"Suppose she never even got the coat?" one boy said gloomily.

"Suppose she got it and didn't like it?" another asked.

"Even if she liked it," I pointed out, "she may not care about us. Why should she? We are nothing to her."

We grew more and more upset and worried. The rumors about the *Aktion* did not stop.

Then one day Mr. Blaugrund called the thirteen of us into his office.

"Please sit down," he said.

We all sat down on the floor. There were not enough chairs to go round.

Mr. Blaugrund smiled and brought out a letter.

"It is from Frau Biebow," he said. He held it up so we could see it. The letter was written in longhand, by her, personally. He read it to us. It was very kind. She thanked each of us by name for her lovely coat. It was truly a surprise, she said. She was very grateful to all of us for remembering her on her birthday.

Then she had a surprise for us in return. She had recommended that we all be sent to the *Heim* for a week.

We were thrilled!

The *Heim* means "home" in German. It was a special place, outside the ghetto walls. Those who had done special duty or earned a reward in some way were sent there. Three days later, we were all taken there.

Out of the nearly 1,000 days I lived in the Lodz Ghetto, those seven days were the happiest. We slept on beds, on fresh, clean sheets. We were given five meals a day with all the bread and meat and fresh fruit we wanted. I had forgotten what meat and fruit tasted like! I remembered six-year-old Herschel asking his mother what a chicken was. The child had been in the ghetto so long he could not remember.

At the *Heim*, we had nothing to do all day long but play. We were almost children again.

For six days I was very happy. But the seventh was torture. I knew that tomorrow I would have to go back to the fear and the cold and the hunger. But for seven days I had had enough to eat. Later, looking back on that time, I know those days gave us children the energy to go on for at least a few more

months. Many were not so lucky.

On the seventh day I returned to my family. I had missed them and they had missed me. No one was bitter or jealous that I had been to this wonderful place. Our family was very close. My parents worked hard to see that we held onto our love and respect for each other. After all, it was the only thing we had left in life. We had seen what happened to families who lost their love for each other because of the terrible strain of the fear and the hunger. We could hear them at night, yelling and screaming and fighting over food.

My father put his arm around me.

"You have done well, Ben," he said quietly. "The rumors have stopped. We believe there will be no *Aktion*."

And there was no *Aktion*, at least not for a while.

Was it because of the coat? Did this simple gift prove to the Nazis that we were productive? Did it prove to them that we had the right to live? To this day I do not know the answer. But I like to think that Frau Biebow said a few words to her husband, the Commandant, that spared the children of the Lodz Ghetto for at least a small period of time.

BEN AND HIS FAMILY MANAGED TO STAY TO-gether in the Lodz Ghetto until it was closed. Others were not so lucky. Little Herschel was discovered and taken from his mother. Rachel, overcome with grief, jumped from a high window in her apartment building and killed herself. But when the ghetto was closed, Ben and his family were herded onto cattle cars and shipped, with thousands of others, to the death camp at Auschwitz. Here, as they got off the train, the Nazis separated the men from the women. This was the last time Ben saw his mother and one of his sisters.

Ben and his father stayed together. They were prisoners at Auschwitz for many days, waiting their turn to die. Finally they were taken to the gas chambers. But as they stood there, a command came through. Their group was to be taken to a forced labor camp. Here, however, Ben's father died, unable to withstand the terrible working conditions.

The Germans saw the end of the war coming. They saw the Allied soldiers advancing. The Nazis tried to kill as many of the Jews as possible. Ben's wife, Dora, who was in Bergen-Belsen, tells one of the ways they used. Before the Nazis left in front of Allied troops, they baked hundreds of loaves of fresh bread and

told the women to eat them. The starving women nearly did so, but a doctor warned them in time that the bread was poisoned.

Ben was put aboard a train, supposedly to be moved away from the danger zone. But the Nazis opened fire on the train with machine guns. They mowed down the Jews crowded aboard, killing hundreds. Ben managed to escape in the darkness, although he was hit in the thigh. A kind farmer took pity on him and hid him for a little while. Ben managed to make it to a road. He collapsed there when he saw a motorcycle approaching. But on the motorcycle was an American doctor who rushed him to a hospital.

The nightmare was over.

Ben was fifteen years old. He weighed sixty pounds.

After the war, Ben found his sister. They were the only two of their large family including aunts, uncles, cousins—to survive.

Out of 160,000 residents of the Lodz Ghetto, only about 1,000 survived the war.

ABOUT THE AUTHOR

MARGARET EDITH (WEIS) BALD-
WIN was born in 1948 in Independence, Missouri. She graduated from the University of
Missouri, Columbia, with a dual degree in Cre-
ative Writing and History. Ms. Baldwin works
for Herald Publishing House as director of the
trade division, Independence Press, and is ad-
vertising director. She has worked for Herald
House for ten years. The author is married to
Robert Baldwin, State Trooper with the Missouri State Highway Patrol,and has two children, David and Elizabeth, and three cats.